# *PARODIES LOST*

*by*

## *Glynn Leaney*

# Parodies Lost

by

## Glynn Leaney

ISBN: 978-0-9929972-0-5

Published by GL Publishing in conjunction with Writersworld. This book is produced entirely in the UK, is available to order from most book shops in the United Kingdom, and is globally available via UK-based Internet book retailers and www.amazon.com.

Copy edited by Ian Large

Cover design and illustrations by Jag Lall

www.writersworld.co.uk

**WRITERSWORLD**
2 Bear Close Flats
Bear Close
Woodstock
Oxfordshire
OX20 1JX
England

☎ 01993 812500
☎ +44 1993 812500

The text pages of this book are produced via an independent certification process that ensures the trees from which the paper is produced come from well-managed sources that exclude the risk of using illegally logged timber while leaving options to use post-consumer recycled paper as well.

# CONTENTS

Introduction   6

## FIFTIES FAVOURITES

INSPIRED BY

All I Ever Do is Scream   Everley Brothers   8
Go and Make My Day   Buddy Holly   9
I'm Lost up This Mountain   Frank Sinatra   10
Oh! Darryl!   Neil Sedaka   11
Reading the News   Guy Mitchell   12
Road Hog   Elvis Presley   13
Swingin' in the Train   Gene Kelly   14
There Goes Summer   Jerry Keller   15
Untrained Comedy   Righteous Brothers   16
When I Call You, Love   Nat King Cole   17
You Get up My Nose   The Platters   18
You Make Me Want to Heave!   Conway Twitty   19
King's New Codes   Danny Kaye   21

## SWINGIN' SIXTIES

(Sittin' in) the Dock All Today   Otis Redding   24
A Waste of Money   Beatles   25
And I Missed Her   Beach Boys   26
Dangers in the Night   Frank Sinatra   27
For Once in Your Life   Stevie Wonder   28
I Want to Join Your Band   Beatles   29
I'm Misbehavin'   Fats Waller   30
I'm Oh So Lonely   Roy Orbison   31
It Hasn't Stopped Raining Since September   Carole King   32
I've Lost all Sense of Feeling   Righteous Brothers   33
Now I'm Sixty-Five   Beatles   34
Larry Popper's Only Arts Club's Banned   Beatles   35
Photo of My Dad   Matt Munro   36
He Loathes You   Beatles   37
Textin' the Day Away   Chubby Checker   38
The Tragic Dull History Tour   Beatles   40
Two Little Girls   Rolf Harris   41
Were You Lonesome Last Night?   Elvis Presley   43
Will He Still be Here Tomorrow?   Shirelles   44
The Flying Instructor   Bob Newhart   46

## MUSICAL MEMENTOS

I Schemed a Scheme   Les Miserables   51
You've No Business in Show Business   Annie Get Your Gun   52
If You Wish to be a Star   Pinocchio   53

| | | |
|---|---|---|
| *Oh Dear Daddy!* | Mama Mia | *54* |
| *The Taxman Takes it All* | Mama Mia | *55* |
| *Street Lighting!* | Grease | *57* |
| *Look at You, You're Dr Who* | Grease | *58* |
| *Hopelessly Dependent on You* | Grease | *59* |
| *You've Got to Take a Wicket or Two* | Oliver | *60* |

## SEVENTIES SPECIALS

| | | |
|---|---|---|
| *And on My Own, Sad to Say* | Gilbert O'Sullivan | *63* |
| *Another Kick in the Teeth* | Pink Floyd | *64* |
| *Bring on the Clouds* | Julie Covington | *65* |
| *Bernie (The Biggest Dustman in the West)* | Benny Hill | *66* |
| *Don't Let My Son be Mad with Me* | Elton John | *68* |
| *My Reputation* | The Who | *69* |
| *Handle on the Team* | Elton John | *70* |
| *I Don't Like Sundays* | Boomtown Rats | *72* |
| *I'm Glad it isn't Christmas Everyday* | Wizzard | *74* |
| *Sixty Ways to Peeve Your Mother* | Simon & Garfunkel | *76* |
| *Porterloo* | ABBA | *77* |
| *Your Friend Dan* | Slade | *78* |
| *Sands of Brighton* | Roger Whittaker | *79* |
| *T-E-R-E-N-C-E* | Dolly Parton | *81* |

## A CHRISTMAS CRACKER

| | | |
|---|---|---|
| *The Day After Christmas* | Clement C Moore | *83* |

## ECSTATIC EIGHTIES

| | | |
|---|---|---|
| *A Winter Sale* | David Essex | *86* |
| *I Guess That's Why They Bring Us the News* | Elton John | *87* |
| *I Want Work* | Elton John | *88* |
| *I Have a Scheme* | ABBA | *89* |
| *I've Just Called to Say I've Left You* | Stevie Wonder | *90* |
| *Logical* | Olivia Newton John | *91* |
| *Running Up My Bill* | Kate Bush | *92* |
| *You Fluff It* | Roy Orbison | *94* |
| *The Great Defender* | Freddie Mercury | *95* |

## AND TO FINISH

| | | |
|---|---|---|
| *Fry me Some Liver* | Michael Buble | *97* |
| *Rain is All Around* | Wet Wet Wet | *98* |
| *I Did it for Me* | Michael Buble | *99* |
| *It's a Terrible Day* | Michael Buble | *100* |
| *You Just Haven't Met Me Yet* | Michael Buble | *102* |

For Kathryn, Christopher and Marc

who have to suffer my humour,

but where would we be without it?

# INTRODUCTION

I first started writing comic verse when I was a boarder at Kirkham Grammar School in Lancashire. We were required to sit in the main hall each evening for a set period to do homework, and were not allowed to leave until the set time was up. Since I often finished my work early, I would then put pen to paper and write poems of various lengths and content. My regret was that when I left school, I tossed everything away!

During my 25 years serving in the Royal Air Force, I expanded my writing to include plays – one full-length and two one-act – as well as numerous scripts for revues, limericks galore, and it was during this time that I fell in love with re-writing the words to pop songs.

During my second career in the financial industry, I expanded into writing children's books, all in verse, and started writing my own songs. Following a successful time on Channel Four's "Countdown", I enjoyed the experience so much that it prompted me to write "Countdown – the Pantomime", a one-act comedy with several parodies that don't appear in this book.

After retiring from the financial world in 2012, it was time to start writing in earnest. For fun I have now completed the task I set myself to totally rewrite "Les Miserables", which now lies dormant in the annals of my office.

"Parodies Lost" is a collection of some of my favourite re-writes, designed for readers who can fit the words to the tune. I hope you enjoy them.

# FIFTIES FAVOURITES

# ALL I EVER DO IS SCREAM

Scream...
Scream, scream, scream,
Scream...
Scream, scream, scream,

When I see you at the school,
The things you do, you're such a fool.
Whenever I see you
All I ever do is scream...
Scream, scream, scream.

The same each day, in the class,
At work or play, you're such an ass.
Whenever I see you
All I ever do is scream...
Scream, scream, scream.
Scream, scream.

I don't like your style,
I could run a mile,
Every time you appear.
You should change your ways,
All ways,
Don't you dare to come near.

When I see you at the school,
The things you do, you're such a fool.
Whenever I see you
All I ever do is scream...
Scream, scream, scream.
Scream...
Scream, scream, scream,
Scream.

# GO AND MAKE MY DAY

Go and make my day, and please say goodbye,
Go and make my day, I'm not going to cry,
I want you now to leave, and that's not a lie,
So go and make my day, say goodbye.

Well, we started off in clover but we know it's over,
Once I started going out with someone new.
Though you used to love me honey,
It was only for my money,
Now I'm glad that we are through.

Go and make my day, and please say goodbye,
Go and make my day, I'm not going to cry,
I want you now to leave, and that's not a lie,
So go and make my day, say goodbye.

Although it breaks your heart, you know we must part,
The time has come at last when you must go.
You say you want to stay but I have to say,
Now's the time and you well know...

Go and make my day, and please say goodbye,
Go and make my day, I'm not going to cry,
I want you now to leave, and that's not a lie,
So go and make my day, say goodbye.

Go and make my day, hoo-hoo
Go make my day, hoo-hoo
Go make my day, hoo-hoo
Go make my day.

# I'M LOST UP THIS MOUNTAIN

I'm lost up this mountain
And I don't know where to go.
All my sherpas have left me,
Now I'm stuck in all this snow.

Three peaks on this mountain,
Each one looking just the same.
Now I'm lost on this mountain,
Only got myself to blame.

How to get myself back home?
How to get myself back home?

I'm lost up this mountain,
And my gear has gone to ground.
If one wish could be granted,
I'd be back home safe and sound.

Please be kind!
Please be kind!
Please be kind!

I'm lost up this mountain
With strange noises all around.
If one wish could be granted,
I'd be back home safe and sound.

Please be kind!
Please be kind!
Please be kind!

## OH! DARRYL!

Oh! Darryl, you are such a fool.
Buddy, you're stupid,
'Cause you think you're cool!
You say things but you often lie,
And then what happens,
I just go and cry.

Buddy, you are really quite a bummer,
And I've told you so.
Don't ever stay here,
Pack your bags and go.
I will never want you as a lover,
No matter what you say.
Oh! Darryl, I wish you'd go away!

Oh! Darryl, you are such a clown,
Buddy, I loathe you when you talk me down.
You say things that you never mean,
You are the worst man I have ever seen!

Buddy, you are really quite a bummer,
And I've told you so.
Don't ever stay here,
Pack your bags and go.
I will never want you as a lover,
No matter what you say.
Oh! Darryl, I wish you'd go away!

## *READING THE NEWS*

Well, I've never felt less like reading the news,
I partied all night, and now full of booze,
No wonder, that I'm feeling this way.

Well, I've never felt less like going on air,
My head's in a spin, and I couldn't care
What's happened; I just hate reading the news.

I don't care if stars keep well away,
For all to leave would make my day,
There's something now that I must do
And that's to find the nearest loo (the nearest loo).

Now I never felt more like staying away,
And feeling like this, well, I couldn't stay
Much longer; you must go reading the news.

I don't care if stars keep well away,
For all to leave would make my day,
There's something now that I must do
And that's to find the nearest loo (the nearest loo).

Now I never felt more like staying away,
And feeling like this, well, I couldn't stay
Much longer; you must go reading the news.

## ROAD HOG

I've never seen such a road hog,
Takin' up the road.
I've never seen such a road hog,
Takin' up the road.
Well, you're a danger to the public,
You ignore the Highway Code.

Now you think you are special,
But I think you're a toad.
Now you think you are special,
But I think you're a toad.
Well, you're a danger to the public,
You ignore the Highway Code.

I've never seen such a road hog,
Takin' up the road.
I've never seen such a road hog,
Takin' up the road.
Well, you're a danger to the public,
You ignore the Highway Code.

## SWINGIN' IN THE TRAIN

Daa-daa-daa-daa
Daa-daa-daa-daa-daa-daa
Daa-daa-daa-daa
Daa-daa-daa-daa-daa-daa...

I'm swingin' in the train,
Just swingin' in the train,
Got a nauseous feelin',
Unhappy again.
I'm crushed in a crowd,
I'm feeling quite rough,
There's ten stops to go,
But I want to get off.

Not a seat to be found,
With my feet on the ground,
I sway side to side,
With the others around.
I'm feeling the strain,
And unhappy again,
Just swingin',
Just swingin' in the train...

Unhappy again...

I'm swingin' and sufferin' in the train...

# THERE GOES SUMMER

There goes summer;
Did you blink and miss the day?
There goes summer;
Need my brolly come what may.
There goes summer;
Roads like rivers every day.
I wish the sun would shine on my poor ol' flooded home.

Now, spring was quite bad but now's no better,
I never had time to get a tan.
Soaked to the skin in the pouring rain,
And they still propose a hosepipe ban!

Oh summer!
There goes summer,
When we met we went indoors.
It was awful;
When it rains it always pours!
I wish the sun would shine on my poor
ol' flooded home.

There goes summer;
All those months, no sun in sight.
There goes summer;
Keep the heat on every night.
And those forecasts,
They are never ever right!
I wish the sun would shine on my poor
ol' flooded home.

Now I want to take my
little boat out
And try to catch a fish or
two.
Go for a punt on the local
river,
End with a pint, well, wouldn't you?

Oh summer!
Has it ever been this bad?

What a bummer!
It's no wonder we're all sad.
It's so crazy,
There's a chance we'll end up mad!
I wish the sun would shine on my poor ol' flooded home.
(I wish the sun would shine…)
Well that was summer for a day!


## UNTRAINED COMEDY

Oh, my God, my goodness,
I can't believe my ears,
So dull, all the time.
You are so unfunny,
You're boring me to tears.
It's such a crime!
We need to laugh, we need to laugh,
Please make us laugh, for me.

Audiences are low,
Can't you see, can't you see?
And they won't improve,
Can't you see?
Audiences all cry,
Then they flee, then they flee,
They're all going home when they flee.

Oh, my God, my goodness,
I can't believe my ears.
So dull, all the time.
You are so unfunny,
You're boring me to tears.
It's such a crime!
We need to laugh, we need to laugh,
Please make us laugh, for me.

## *WHEN I CALL YOU, LOVE*

When I call you, love,
Please be there and waiting,
Or I'll never call you, love.
In this tiresome world we live in,
I'm fed up when you're never there.
And it seems you don't want to answer,
So I guess that you don't really care.

Since I waste my time,
Don't know why I bother,
So I'll stop now wasting time.
And the moment that I feel that
You feel that we're through,
Is when I stop all calls to you.

And the moment that I feel that
You feel that we're through,
Is when I stop all calls to you.

## YOU GET UP MY NOSE

They wondered what was wrong,
I knew all along.
People stop and sigh,
Others start to cry
When you tell a lie.

They caught on right away
And I have to say,
Everyone now knows
How the saying goes,
You get up my nose.

Things you do we always see right through,
And things you go and say.
Soon you'll find you'll get no peace of mind,
You'll never get your way.

You have no friends at all,
Feeling rather small,
Knowing I suppose
How the saying goes,
You get up my nose.

You get up my nose.

## YOU MAKE ME WANT TO HEAVE!

You annoy us everywhere,
Each time you stop and stare,
People run, they try to leave,
You know you make me want to heave!

My one and only fear,
Is that you'll get too near,
As everything you do
Makes everybody blue.
I'm sure by now you know,
How much we loathe you so.
My hope is that you'll see
Just what you do to me.
You make me want to heave.

Yes, everything you do
Is far away untrue.
Your thoughts, your words, your deeds,
You have no real needs.
Your mind you can't control,
It rules your very soul.
My hope is that you'll see
Just what you do to me.
You make me want to heave.

My one and only fear,
Is that you'll get too near,
As everything you do
Makes everybody blue.
I'm sure by now you know,
How much we loathe you so.
My hope is that you'll see
Just what you do to me.
Only you make me want to heave.

In the mid 1970s, whilst serving in the Royal Air Force as an administrative officer, I was posted to the Royal Air Force Personnel Management Centre (PMC) where service personnel worked alongside civilians designing and maintaining computer programmes. It was in the early days of huge computers, punch-tape and the most basic of computer languages.

In my job as a maintenance programmer, I worked in a large office where I was the only serving RAF member. They were fun days and the camaraderie among those in the office was tremendous. The day's work was broken each morning and afternoon by the appearance of Annie with her trolley full of goodies. It made a welcome break to the daily grind.

By now I was well into writing comic verse and enjoying listening to comedy, and in particular humorous monologues. Back in 1952, Danny Kaye recorded "The King's New Clothes", and I knew the song well. In our office was a colleague called Andy King who was also in the business of writing computer codes. It was too good an opportunity to miss and it was over 35 years ago that I decided to produce my own version of "King's New Codes".

I dedicate this to Andy and to all those with whom I worked at the time.

# KING'S NEW CODES

This is the story of King's new codes.

Once upon a time there was a young computer programmer called King. Now, one day King was instructed to produce a new set of codes for the pay review, given to him by the big boss himself – Big G. After spending many long hours and earning much overtime, King produced a big binder full of empty foolscap pages, presented it to Big G and said:

"Sir, here is your new set of codes. This, however, is no ordinary set of codes, but a magic set that has cost me a lot of effort." King went on to explain: "To a fool, it appears that there's nothing on the paper at all. But to an ambitious, switched-on officer with thoughts on his next annual report, this is the most fantastic set of codes ever produced."

Well, naturally, not wanting to appear a fool, Big G bellowed, "Isn't it neat, isn't it fine, look at the code on every line!

This set of codes is altogether but altogether it's altogether and altogether the finest set of codes I've ever seen. The pages here are bound in leather; I don't know whether if I have ever seen anything like it before in my life, the best I've ever seen. Call the wing commanders!"...and very soon they convened.

Now as soon as the wing commanders were standing rigid to attention, eyes peering over the top of the desk in Big G's office, King hurriedly explained to them about the magic set of codes.

Well, naturally, this dynamic duo with ideas of possible promotion, and not wanting to appear fools, stuttered, "Look at the text, look at the style, must be the best in the airmen's file...

This set of codes is altogether but altogether it's altogether and altogether the finest set of codes we've ever seen. Results will show there's nothing better; we don't know whether if we have ever seen anything like it before in our lives, the best we've ever seen. Call the entire department"...in the conference room they convened.

Well, within minutes the entire department had rushed to the conference room. All the section leaders were there, the programmers with their task sheets were there, maxtesters, protesters, clerical assistants and typists were there. All had assembled and were quickly told about the magic set of codes.

Well, naturally, not wanting to appear fools, they exclaimed, "Isn't it oooh, isn't it aaah, isn't it absolutely wheee!...

This set of codes is altogether but altogether it's altogether and altogether the finest set of codes we've ever seen. This work results from dedication, an inspiration, a mild sensation, this new creation should now be seen by all at the PMC. Get them all assembled, including the AOC."

And so it was that the entire Personnel Management Centre staff was told about the magic set of codes. One by one, members filed past and gasped in amazement at the leather-bound pages...all that is except Annie with her trolley. You see, Annie had been too occupied to hear about the magic set of codes and, unaware of what she was supposed to see, when she saw the blank pages cried out:

"Look at this thing, look at this thing, look at this thing, this thing, this thing!

This set of codes is altogether but altogether it's altogether and altogether as empty as the rolls I try to sell. I don't find this at all exciting, it's not the lighting, there is no writing, I think it's frightening to think that you've been taken in as well."

The entire civil service suddenly got nervous, they suddenly found themselves wide open to ridicule and scorn. Now King is in the altogether but altogether is altogether and altogether as junior as the day that he was born, and all hopes of future promotion are all forlorn!

# SWINGIN' SIXTIES

## (SITTIN' IN) THE DOCK ALL TODAY

Sittin' in the local court,
I've been wishin' that I hadn't been caught.
Seeing the judge roll in,
And then I see the jury come in again, yeah.

I'm sittin' in the dock all today,
Hoping that things go my way.
Ooh, I'm just sittin' in the dock all today,
Killing time.

I robbed a bank in Goring,
Thought that I'd get clean away.
But I slipped on the flooring,
I suppose you'd say it wasn't my day!

And now I've had to sit in the dock all today,
Hoping that things go my way.
Ooh, I'm sittin' in the dock all today,
Killing time.

Seems like things are going to change,
Just as soon as I'm in a cell.
I daren't think what the inmates want me to do,
But I guess my life will be hell, yes.

Sittin' here shocked to the core,
And I don't think I can take any more.
Never had a chance of bail,
Going from this dock to jail.

Well I've now finished in this dock, and from today
Biding my lifetime away,
And my hair has started going grey,
Doing time.

# A WASTE OF MONEY

A waste of money... wasting my savings and time.

I spent a fortune on a cruise,
It looked so good, I couldn't lose;
A waste of money... wasting my savings and time.

I won't return, no I won't return,
I'll go back for my money and sue.

The trip I took seemed so safe and sound,
The ruddy ship went and ran aground,
A waste of money... wasting my savings and time.

I won't return, no I won't return,

I'll go back (he'll go back)
For my money (for his money)
And sue.

## AND I MISSED HER

Well I picked up the phone and asked her if she wanted to meet.
She sounded so nice and I guessed she must have been rather sweet.
So we went and made a date,
Should have been at half past eight,
But as it was I turned up late
And I missed her.

Each time I phoned her I told her just how sorry I'd been.
I wanted to make it up, well you know what I mean.
We made another date and then,
I made a note of where and when.
Would you believe I was late again,
And so I missed her.

I missed her and it's hard as I've never missed a date before.
I missed her and it's hard as it left me feeling rather sore.

I'd give it one more time so I called her with a plea from my heart.
I told her that once we met we'd never then be apart.
So we fixed a new date and time,
It was meant to be sublime,
But I was late, oh what a crime!
And so I missed her.

And so I missed her.
And so I missed her.

## DANGERS IN THE NIGHT

Dangers in the night,
That's what I call men.
Often I take fright,
And that's not all, when-
Ever they're in sight, I turn my back and run.

If I stopped to fight,
They'd leave me crying.
And you know they might
Just leave me sighing,
Turn off every light, and then have lots of fun.

Dangers in the night,
To all and sundry
These men make love every night...
Except on Sunday when we say a little prayer,
Wondering if they care,
Knowing that one little error could result in holy terror.

Ever since one night,
I've been expecting.
What a sorry plight,
I'm now suspecting
Things did not go right with dangers in the night!

## FOR ONCE IN YOUR LIFE

For once in your life can't you do something useful,
Something to make us all smile.
For once I'm afraid, you can never be truthful,
I know it isn't your style.

For once I could pray that you'd do something different,
Something good as well.
Far as I can tell,
There's not a hope in hell!

For once in your life say some words that won't hurt me,
Because you've hurt me before.
For once I just wish you would go and desert me,
Don't want you round anymore.

For once you can say what you want, I won't listen,
The sooner you walk out my life I'll be wishin'
For once and for all, I'll have no-one needling me.

## I WANT TO JOIN YOUR BAND

Oh yeah I've heard from someone that you are under-manned,
So I can be that someone, I want to join your band.
I want to join your band; I want to join your band.

Oh please look at me and say that I'm your man,
And please say to me you'll let me join your band.
You'll let me join your band; you'll let me join your band.

And if I join you I will hope you'd agree,
I'd be an asset to your band,
You will see, you will see, you will see!

Yeah, I've got that something,
It's known throughout the land.
And I'll show you something,
If I can join your band.
I want to join your band,
I want to join your band,
I want to join your band.

## I'M MISBEHAVIN'

I'm feelin' naughty
Here on my own;
I'm feelin' sporty
Though I'm sittin' all alone.
I'm misbehavin'
I'm blamin' what I do on you.

One thing for certain,
I'll have my day,
And now I'm blirtin'
I've got loads of things to say.
I'm misbehavin'
I'm blamin' what I do on you.

Feelin' horny,
And it's corny.
Can't go nowhere,
But do I care?
My missus aint worth waitin' for...
Believe me.

I just stay in now,
Don't need to go.
I have the know-how,
It's time I put on a show.
I'm misbehavin'
I'm blamin' what I do on you.

# I'M OH SO LONELY

Dum-dum-dum-dumdy-doo-wah,
Ooh-yay-yay-yay-yeah,
Oh-oh-oh-oh-wah,
I'm oh so lonely.

I'm oh so lonely (dum-dum-dum-dumdy-doo-wah),
As I'm on my own tonight (ooh-yay-yay-yay-yeah).
I'm oh so lonely (dum-dum-dum-dumdy-doo-wah),
Think I'll go and get tight (dum-dum-dum-dumdy-doo-wah).

Where is my lady? Where is my heart?
She's gone and left me; called me a fart!

So now I'm so lonely, and now I cry,
As I'm so lonely.

Dum-dum-dum-dumdy-doo-wah,
Ooh-yay-yay-yay-yeah,
Oh-oh-oh-oh-wah,
I'm oh so lonely.

I'm oh so lonely (dum-dum-dum-dumdy-doo-wah),
It's no wonder I feel blue (ooh-yay-yay-yay-yeah).
I'm oh so lonely (dum-dum-dum-dumdy-doo-wah),
And I blame it all on you (dum-dum-dum-dumdy-doo-wah).

And now I'm thinking, get in my car.
I'll go drinking in a new bar; find someone new,
As I know I've lost you.
I'm oh so lonely.

Dum-dum-dum-dumdy-doo-wah.

# IT HASN'T STOPPED RAINING SINCE SEPTEMBER

What should I write?
What can I do?
What can I say about our dreadful weather?

The rain we've had has been as bad as it can be.
It's been disastrous for the likes of you and me.
We haven't seen the sun forever and a day,
As it hasn't stopped raining since September.

We need some sunny days with skies not grey but blue.
It's not just countryside that's soaked the whole way through.
My house is flooded and I've moved quite far away,
As it hasn't stopped raining since September.

We all look forward to a summer with some sun,
As everybody hates this awful rain.
The non-stop downpour has affected everyone.
This climate change is just a ruddy pain!

It really bugs me that the skies are always grey.
We need a miracle to chase the clouds away.
I'm looking forward to the time when skies are blue,
As it hasn't stopped raining since September.
September, September, oh
It hasn't stopped raining since September.

## I'VE LOST ALL SENSE OF FEELING

I always close my eyes every time that you come so near,
And there is bitterness in your heart as you shed a tear.
I try so hard not to scold you, baby,
But baby, baby I told you

I've lost all sense of feeling,
Yes all my sense of feeling.
I've lost all sense of feeling,
And it's long, long, gone, oh oh oh.

Now I've no happiness in my heart when you reach for me,
And can't you tell since we've been apart I feel better free.
I feel it hard to stop smiling, baby,
'Cause baby, it is now not surprising.

I've lost all sense of feeling,
Yes all my sense of feeling.
I've lost all sense of feeling,
And it's long, long, gone, oh oh oh.

Baby, baby, I'd go right now if I were you,
Since I can't love you at all like I used to do.
There is no love, no love, no love that we had once before;
It's gone, gone, gone, don't ask any more.

Baby, baby, baby, baby
Baby please, please, baby please...

I've lost all sense of feeling,
Yes all my sense of feeling.
I've lost all sense of feeling,
And it's long, long, gone,
And we can't go on, no oh oh.

## NOW I'M SIXTY-FIVE

Now that I'm older, lost all my hair, wondering what to do.
Should I keep on working in the same old way?
Go part time? Or call it a day?

Money's no problem, whatever comes in; it's all spent by the wife.
So do I keep scheming? Or am I just dreaming,
Now I'm sixty-five.

What are my options? How do I choose, when all's said and done?
A lie-in every morning seems a good idea,
And tea in bed? The wife says, "No fear!"

Reading the papers, watching TV, I'd like an easy life.
But am I just dreaming, or do I keep scheming,
Now I'm sixty-five.

If I gave up working I just know
there'd be no shirking
With the jobs I'd have to do.
Housework isn't quite my scene.
Washing, ironing and cleaning loos,
I find it all obscene!

Here's the solution, a small
compromise – just work now and
then.
We can keep on going as we did
before,
I roll it in... the wife then spends
more.

Why am I worried? There's no need at all.
I'm happy with my life.
I'm done with the scheming, positively beaming,
Now I'm sixty-five.

## LARRY POPPER'S ONLY ARTS CLUB'S BANNNED

It was in the Easter break last year,
Larry Popper had a great idea.
He was drinking in his local pub,
When he thought about a brand new club,

But now we have to break the news,
A fact that's brought on lots of tears.
Larry Popper's only arts club's banned!

Poor Larry Popper's only arts club's banned,
We think that it's a crying shame.
Larry Popper's only arts club's banned;
We want to find out who's to blame.
Larry Popper's arts club, Larry Popper's arts club,
Larry Popper's only arts club's banned.

The club was really buzzing
With people posing nude.
It had a growing membership,
They liked to show their portraits off,
They loved to take them home.

And now someone's gone and closed it down,
But the news is going round the town,
That the members will start up anew,
So it seems there's hope for me and you.
And if you really do like art,
There's every reason to take heart,
Though Larry Popper's only arts club's banned.

## PHOTO OF MY DAD

I have never seen a picture of my Dad,
For he has been inside for years.
No-one's ever seen a picture of my Dad,
But I'm not shedding any tears.

Anyone who knew him, had no problem seeing
through him.

He'll be home one day, and if I had my way,
He'd start to lead a better life,
And try to make us glad,
And then I'll take a photo of my Dad!

He'll be home one day, and if I had my way,
He'd start to lead a better life,
And try to make us glad,
And then I'll take a photo of my Dad!

## HE LOATHES YOU

He loathes you, nah, nah, nah,
He loathes you, nah, nah, nah,
He loathes you, nah, nah, nah, nah.

You think you found new love but I saw him just today.
It's Sue he's thinking of and he told me not to say…
That he loathes you and you know that must be bad.
He loathes you, I suppose that makes you sad.

He said you ought to know that he likes the girl called Sue.
It's over now and so you're going to feel quite blue,
Because he loathes you and you know that must be bad.
He loathes you, I suppose that makes you sad.

He loathes you, nah, nah, nah,
He loathes you, nah, nah, nah,
A rebuff like that, you know it must be bad.

And now it's up to you, though you think it's most unfair,
The best thing you can do is forget he's ever there.
Because he loathes you and you know that must be bad.
He loathes you, I suppose that makes you sad.

He loathes you, nah, nah, nah,
He loathes you, nah, nah, nah,
A rebuff like that, you know it must be bad.
A rebuff like that, you know it must be bad.
A rebuff like that, you know it must be bad.

Nah, nah, nah, nah, nah, nah,
Nah, nah, nah, nah.

# TEXTIN' THE DAY AWAY

Let me tell you 'bout a craze
Started back in techie days.
Now I'm going through a phase
Textin' the day away.
Cheaper than to make a call,
Everyone can have a ball.
Available to one and all,
Textin' the day away.

We're textin', textin',
No limit on what you say.
We're textin', textin',
We're textin' the day away.

Here's a girl who ain't no fool,
She just likes to play it cool.
Now she spends her day at school
Textin' the day away.
Laughing at the things she says
And it seems she has no cares.
What she does she does with flare,
Textin' the day away.

We're textin', textin',
No limit on what you say.
We're textin', textin',
We're textin' the day away.

Let's text a while.
Push up,
Push down,
Push up,

Push down,
Wanabe.
Now start,
Now text,
We're textin' the day away.

Here's a boy who knows his trade,
He knows when he's got it made.
He will never be afraid
Textin' the day away.

Wow, you ought to see him go,
Hittin' digits high and low.
What he says we'll never know,
Textin' the day away.

We're textin', textin',
No limit on what you say.
We're textin', textin',
We're textin' the day away.

Let's text a while.
Push up,
Push down,
Push up,
Push down,
Wanabe.
Now start,
Now text,
We're textin' the day away.

# THE TRAGIC DULL HISTORY TOUR

Roll up, for the tragic dull history tour.
Roll up, for the tragic dull history tour.
Roll up, you need no invitation, for the tragic dull history tour.
Roll up, we start from Kings Cross station,
For the tragic dull history tour.

The tragic dull history tour is waiting to bore you today,
Waiting to bore you today.

Roll up, for the tragic dull history tour.
Roll up, for the tragic dull history tour.

Roll up, there's not a lot you need, for the tragic dull history tour.
Roll up, there's nothing guaranteed, in the tragic dull history tour.
The tragic dull history tour is waiting to bore you today,
Waiting to bore you today.

A history trip.
The tragic dull history tour.

Roll up, for the tragic dull history tour.
Roll up, you need no invitation, for the tragic dull history tour.
Roll up, we start from Kings Cross Station,
For the tragic dull history tour.

The tragic dull history tour is waiting to bore you today,
Waiting to bore you today.
The tragic dull history tour is waiting to bore you today,
Dying to bore you today, bore you today.

## TWO LITTLE GIRLS

Two little girls had beautiful curls,
Each had a two-wheeled bike.
Daily they rode out on the road,
Crazy as you like.
One of the pair then flew through the air,
Fell on her little head.
Wiping her eye she started to cry,
When her young sister said...

Don't you think I just love you crying;
There's no room on my bike for two.
Stay down there Jill, and keep on crying,
There's no way I can share with you.
When we grow up we'll both be nurses
And our hair will have lost their curls.
And I wonder if we'll remember
When we were two little girls.

Years passed by, each heaved a sigh,
Neither could find employ.
Both bought a car, went to a bar,
Trying to find a boy.
One winter's night, one girl had a fright,
Crashed in a ditch in snow.
Started to cry and thought she would die,
Then heard a voice she'd know…

Don't you think I just love you crying;
I recall what you said before.
You're all right Jean, not really dying,
You can now get up off the floor.

I shall call out the rescue service,
And we'll soon find out what unfurls.
But I hope now that you remember
When we were two little girls.

Don't you think I just love you crying;
I recall what you said before.
You're all right Jean, not really dying,
You can now get up off the floor.
I shall call out the rescue service
And we'll soon find out what unfurls.
But I hope now that you remember
When we were two little girls.

## WERE YOU LONESOME LAST NIGHT?

Were you lonesome last night?
If you were, serves you right.
It's no wonder we drifted apart.
When I think what you said as I fell out of the bed,
And you sat up and called me a fart!

Do you wish I was with you still naked and bare?
Do you look in the mirror and find I'm not there?
Is your head racked with guilt, when you throw back the quilt?
So my dear, were you lonesome last night?

I guess that you were lonesome last night.
You know my mate said you strung me along
And acted all the time.
You had me on a long lead, no reason or rhyme.
The first time that we met I loved your long blond hair.
You played your part convincingly, I fell for it right there.
But very soon you lied to me, and then I could see
That you loved someone else.
Sweetheart, I knew that you never loved me,
It was clear to me from the start.
But I thought I'd enjoy it while I could
Even though I knew we would part.
Now your flat is bare and you're sitting there
With knowing I've gone for good.
I thought I might return one day
But I knew that I never would.

Do you now feel the pain? You won't see me again.
So my dear, were you lonesome last night?

# WILL HE STILL BE HERE TOMORROW?

Tonight his team lost badly.
They face the drop now, sadly.
Tonight the fight is over now for sure.
So will he be here tomorrow?

Was this the final straw now?
And is he on the floor now?
I seem to think he can't take any more.
Will he still be here tomorrow?

Tonight some words were spoken,
He thought he was the chosen one.
But now his contract's broken,
He'll be off in the morning sun.

Although we feel much sorrow,
We'd like to know who follows?
For one thing's sure, our man is on his way,
And he won't be here tomorrow!

For one thing's sure, our man is on his way,
And he won't be here tomorrow!

*When I went through the Royal Air Force College, Cranwell, in the 1960s, although training to become an administrative officer, along with everyone else I learned to fly in a chipmunk, a very light aircraft.*

*Doing the comedy rounds at the time was Bob Newhart with a variety of monologues, one of which was "The Driving Instructor" – a classic still to this day.*

*It didn't take me long to see the potential for a re-write, especially as I was never going to be an ace pilot!*

*And so it was, almost 50 years ago that I put pen to paper to pair up cadet Jenkins with "The Flying Instructor".*

## THE FLYING INSTRUCTOR

Good morning. It's cadet Jenkins, isn't it?... Ah good, well I'm Flight Lieutenant Bird, your new flying instructor. From what I gather you've had several instructors before, right?... Twenty-seven? Oh, I didn't realise it was quite that many... Yes, I do know you're having a little difficulty. Everybody has a little difficulty at the beginning.

Now let me see, have you got your flying log book with you?... Er, oh, all three of them, good. Do you mind if I have a look...thank you...hmmm. I see you've flown quite a few hours without actually going solo yet...two hundred and forty one...oh, and a half, yes well, what's that?... Yes I agree, it's not usual to take that long before going solo, but we're not all born fliers are we. It just takes some people a little longer than others, and in your case, hmmm...

Let's strap ourselves in shall we...yes, the parachute is heavy, isn't it...what's that?... At least you feel safe wearing it. Well of course, they're practically 100% sure to open...oh, you did? You packed it yourself. Ha, ha, well as long as you didn't pack mine I guess one of us will be all right, heh?... Oh, you did! Er, perhaps we won't have to wear them, eh!

Now then, do you know how to taxi the plane to the runway?... You do, good. In that case I'll just sit back and watch and when we're at the end of the runway, you stop and I'll see if there's anything to criticise. OK?... Good. Start her up then...

OK, you can stop it right here. Now that wasn't too bad at all. Just a couple of minor points. First, you really should have allowed that airman to get away with the chocks before starting off... I know he's only a senior aircraftman, but fair's fair, you should have given him a chance to get from under the plane. Secondly, don't you think you were taxiing a little too fast?... Yes, I appreciate you're eager to get up in the air, but 78 knots is a little too fast to taxi, especially in this wind.

Pardon, what's that?... At least we've made it this far. I should hope so. Why, shouldn't we have done?... Oh I see, nineteen of the twenty seven didn't even make it to here! Guess I'm luckier than the average instructor, eh. Well, since we are here, we might as well take off. You do know how to take off, don't you?... You've done it hundreds of times, good...what's that?... Mainly during taxiing. Yes, well that's understandable the speed you taxi! Anyway, take her away.

Good, we're rolling along just fine but, er, why not use the runway?... You prefer a grass take-off! I suppose that's as good a reason as any. I think you ought to be pulling up on the stick now Jenkins. Er, we really ought to be off the deck by now...er, Jenkins, there's a hedge up in front of us and I, I think er, JENKINS, for God's sake!... I didn't think we were going to make it over that hedge...yes, you did prove me wrong... What's that?... You were just testing out my nerves! Ha, ha!

OK, so let's climb above those trees ahead (cough)... Well, I didn't think you were experienced enough to fly between those two trees but...yes, there were a good six inches on either side but all the same I, I...no we won't do it again to prove it wasn't a fluke!... Now, take her up to 5,000 feet without any aerobatics...now that's fine. Just keep her in a steady climb... Good, now level out and try some straight and level.

Before coming to see you, I didn't have time to read your last instructor's report, but I have it right with me so while you just keep flying straight, I'll have a quick look at it. I see that your last instructor wasn't with you very long...seventeen minutes from the time he strapped himself in. I see. Er, what height were you at when he jumped out?... 20,000 feet? That...that's fairly high for a chipmunk isn't it?... The what?... Oh, the captain of the airliner thought so too! Yes, I guess he would. I guess anyone could.

Anyway, you've been doing well for the last couple of minutes keeping us at er, oh, I see we're at 6,000 feet now, but that's OK. I think we ought to try a few aerobatics. I should imagine at this height you should be quite safe to do a barrel roll. Have you done one before?... You...you've done half of one! Do you mind explaining how you managed half a barrel roll?... Oh, I see. You weren't strapped in properly! Presumably the parachute opened all right?... Good.

Well, OK, since you are strapped in tight now, see if you can do a right to left barrel roll… Now that wasn't too bad at all. Um, let's do it to the Air Force right now, shall we?… That's right, the starboard wing to drop first. That's better, but not too fast now… Yes, that was pretty good even if it was a little fast…what's that?… You reckon you can do it faster! Well I'm sorry, you're not supposed to… Hey, cut it out or you'll land up…stop rolling it will you! Jenkins…Jenkins. Are you still with us? Jenkins, stop moaning will you. What?… No, they're not the green fields of paradise. You've still got us upside down! OK, I've got it. There, now we're straight again.

We'll just have another minute or two of straight and level while you have a breather and then…pardon?…you want to go where?… Why didn't you go before you got to the plane?… I know these straps are a nuisance, but they're even more of a nuisance up here!… What's that?… No, that's not what the brown paper bags are for. You'll just have to wait till we land. Tighten your straps!

Now then, I think we'll do a loop. Have you ever…don't tell me you've done only half a loop…you've completed one! Good… Oh, it was the instructor who didn't manage to finish it… You did what?… You tried catching him in the final phase of the loop! What happened?… Yes, the blades do make a nasty mess when they get tangled with the chute!

Well anyway, let's take her up a little…fine. Now push the stick forward and down we go. That's a good start. OK, you can start easing her back… Jenkins, start pulling the stick back…pull her back, Jenkins…JENKINS, for God's sake pull the stick back!… I have control…let go! Whew, I thought − same to you farmer! − I really thought we'd had it then. I think we ought to go back to base… You want to take her home?… Well, OK, you have control again.

After what we've been through, shall I land it?… You think you can manage it. Well, OK, easy does it. Try and line her up with the centre of the runway…that's looking good. Approach is fine…now just a little lower…a little lower…OK touch down, oops, don't worry. Down again. Er, oh dear, third time lucky? Oops, what's that?… You feel like a kangaroo! Funny, Air Traffic have just said we look like one! Not to worry. Since we're doing another circuit you'll have more time to practise.

We're coming round again on final approach and, oh dear, looks like someone's about to take off. Take her up again Jenkins... Jenkins, did you hear me? There's another aircraft just starting off and...Jenkins, we can't land now... What?... No we don't have right of way... JENKINS! We...we missed him?

Well I don't know how we did that but, hey, we've landed too. I was so tense up there that I didn't even realise that...pardon?... Yes, I can see those MPs coming over in their jeep and...yes, they do look pretty cross don't they! (shouts)... What's that?... Well we missed him, didn't we?

Er, Jenkins, I have to go along with these men now. I'll be making my report and...pardon?... Will I recommend you for fast jets??? Aaaaaaaagh!

# MUSICAL
# MEMENTOS

# I SCHEMED A SCHEME

I had a scheme some years ago,
My hopes were high for making money.
I schemed so much and hoped to show
That life for me would turn out sunny.
But I was young and quite naïve,
My plans were made and then rejected.
What could I then hope to achieve;
All hope seemed gone, I was dejected.

But more thoughts came to my head,
I could hear a clap of thunder,
And when lightning struck as well,
I dispelled all thoughts of shame.

I kept a notebook at my side,
I filled each page with awe and wonder.
I took it all within my stride,
And it was done when summer came.

But still my scheme lies in my drawer,
They say it doesn't meet compliance.
I'll have to think a little more,
To get it past the FCA A..A..A..A..

I had a scheme my life would change,
Much different from the pay I'm
earning,
Much different now from what I
dreamed,
But laws have scotched the scheme I
schemed.

## YOU'VE NO BUSINESS IN SHOW BUSINESS

The actors, the stage craft, the smash hits, awards,
Directors who can turn you into stars.
The good guys, the bad guys, the beauties, the broads,
And those who simply hang around in bars.
The first night when you hope it all goes well,
And critics who will often give it hell!

You've no business in show business,
You've no business you know.
Everything about you is appalling!
Everything you say is quite absurd!
Who knows how you ever got the calling,
I find it galling, have you not heard...

You've no talent and you haven't
A chance here on this show.
Yesterday you told us you could dance and sing
Like Fred Astaire and our old friend Bing.
Now today we find that you can't do a thing,
So why don't you just go!

The gangsters, the mobsters, assassins, the molls,
The cops who always seem to get their man.
The monsters, the vampires, the aliens, the trolls,
They'll take you to the cleaners if they can.
The animals that take you for a ride,
The children who you simply can't abide.

You've no business in show business,
And we've told you it's so.
You appear to think that you are charming,
Sweeping all the ladies off the floor.
I can tell you that it's quite alarming,
You're only harming yourself the more.
You've no talent and you haven't
A chance here on this show.
There's no chance that you will ever make the grade,
Of that I'm certain, but I'm afraid
You still think you're something and you've got it made,
But I beg you to go,
And we'll get on with the show!

## IF YOU WISH TO BE A STAR

If you wish to be a star
It's a case of who you are,
Parents with their names in lights
Will help your cause.

People in the know will say
Casting couches show the way!
Having what it takes will help
To open doors.

Life is hard,
It brings rewards to those
Who reach out for success,
And make it happen.

If your heart is really true,
Your resolve will see you through.
If you wish to be a star,
It's up to you.

## OH DEAR DADDY!

You've been cheating on Mum for a number of years,
She's now out of her mind; can't you see all her tears?
Look at her now, won't you ever learn?
You don't know how, and she's going to lose her mind,
You're just nasty and so unkind.
Take a look at yourself and you'll see
What you've done to my mum and to me, w-o-o-o-oh.

Oh dear Daddy, there you go again,
Oh my, none of them resist you.
Oh dear Daddy, at a low again,
Oh my, how many have kissed you?
Now we're both left in limbo,
Since you went with that bimbo.
Bye bye, now it's time for you to go.
Oh dear Daddy, I suppose you know
We'll cry, but it's time for you to go.

Mum just wants to know why; is it something she's done?
She does nothing but cry; did you stop having fun?
It's not just her, but I'm hurting too,
You've caused a stir, but it's time you walked out the door,
You're not welcome here anymore.
Just one look at yourself and you'll see
What you've done to my mum and to me, w-o-o-o-oh

Oh dear Daddy, there you go again,
Oh my, none of them resist you.
Oh dear Daddy, at a low again,
Oh my, how many have kissed you?
Now we're both left in limbo,
Since you went with that bimbo.
Bye bye, now it's time for you to go.
Oh dear Daddy, I suppose you know
We'll cry, but it's time for you to go.

## THE TAXMAN TAKES IT ALL

I've just got to talk
About the state I'm in now.
Going on so long,
It's oh so very wrong.
I have worked so hard,
And I guess you have too.
What more can I say,
When I get my pay...

The taxman takes it all;
I'm left with bugger all.
We've seen it all before,
Always wanting more.

When I started out
I was young and happy.
I worked hard at my school,
Everything was cool.
Passing my exams,
Hoping to do better.
Nothing then to fear,
With a good career.

Then Fate would play a part;
It happened from the start.
I went and lost my way,
And with it went my pay.
The taxman takes it all,
I'm up against a wall.
There's nothing else to gain,
Might as well complain.

I don't know what to do.
Do you have an answer?
Are you just the same,
A number, not a name?
Something deep inside
Tells me I'm a loser.
And so I'm afraid
Tax bill must be paid.

The system isn't fair,
And no-one seems to care.
That's why we're all so poor,
Can't take any more.
The bill arrived today;
I don't know what to say.
The figure isn't small;
The taxman takes it all.

I've just got to talk,
Though I'm feeling so sad.
You can understand,
The same throughout the land.
Don't apologise
If you don't feel sorry.
I feel very weak
As I'm up the creek!
Don't you know
The taxman takes it all
The taxman takes it all...

## *STREET LIGHTING!*

Well this bar is problematic, it's not ecstatic, nor charismatic,
There's no street lighting!

We need to get the local council to splash out on some lights,
oh yeah,
Keep walkin', just keep walkin'.
Danger's all around us, especially at night, oh yeah,
We'll get the lighting, we've got to get the lighting.
Though the council claims it's poor, we'll be knocking on their
door,
It's enough to make you spit but we're never goin' to quit for
street lighting.

No street lighting, you're needed for a quarter mile;
Street lighting, no street lighting.
No street lighting, to have it makes it all worthwhile;
Street lighting, no street lighting.
It's not a dream, the people all scream for street lighting.

We need to make more improvements with benches and
seats, oh yeah,
A modern looking pub and a place to get some eats, oh yeah.
Get the council off their bums; we can then see what comes,
The place will be much better, when we know we're goin' to
get some street lighting.

No street lighting, you're needed for a quarter mile;
Street lighting, no street lighting.
No street lighting, to have it makes it all worthwhile;
Street lighting, no street lighting.
It's not a dream, the people all scream for street lighting.

# LOOK AT YOU, YOU'RE DR WHO

(Looking in the mirror) Look at you, you're Dr Who.
Where you go, you've not a clue.
Won't find a friend who will stay to the end,
I can't, I'm Dr Who.

Look out! There, I'm Fred Astaire,
Dancing round without a care.
Out of the blue all the ladies would queue
To dance with Fred Astaire.

I can laugh (yes) and cry (yes),
I can even fly.
My screwdriver keeps me from harm.
When flying through space
Then it's hard to keep pace,
But you know that I always keep calm.

As for those I call my foes,
They're all afraid, for Heaven knows,
One look at me and they all turn and flee
Because I'm Dr Who.

Two hearts here, you know that's true,
One for me and one for you.
In time and space I'm all over the place;
Look at me, I'm Dr Who!

## HOPELESSLY DEPENDENT ON YOU

Guess I'm the only one who's willing
To tell you just what's on my mind.
I'm not the first, you know
But I am going to show to you...

That though I try to do things my way,
And try to do them on my own.
But even if I could,
It's true I really should have known,
I'm hopelessly dependent on you.

I'm now in over my head,
Is it something that I said?
Oh, I'm feeling blue,
Hopelessly dependent on you,
Hopelessly dependent on you,
Hopelessly dependent on you.

My mum is saying, "Just forget it",
My dad is saying, "Not a clue!"
What then should I try, would I ever die for you?
Hopelessly dependent on you.

I'm now in over my head,
Is it something that I said?
Oh, I'm feeling blue,
Hopelessly dependent on you,
Hopelessly dependent on you,
Hopelessly dependent on you.

# YOU'VE GOT TO TAKE A WICKET OR TWO

In this game, one must win,
Losing counts as a sin;
When it's your turn to take the field,
You've got to take a wicket or two...
You've got to take a wicket or two, boys;
You've got to take a wicket or two.

When you have to take the field,
You've got to take a wicket or two.

Never mind what your score,
There's a need to do more.
Better to get some victims fast
Better take a wicket or two...
You'd better take a wicket or two, boys;
You'd better take a wicket or two.

Need to get some victims fast.
Better take a wicket or two.

When you play in a test,
Got to be at your best.
Whether you're bowling quick or spin,
You've got to take a wicket or two...
You've got to take a wicket or two, boys;
You've got to take a wicket or two.

When you're bowling quick or spin,
You've got to take a wicket or two.

One-day games, they're quite hard,
Need to be on your guard.
Limited time to show who's best,
You've got to take a wicket or two...
You've got to take a wicket or two, boys;
You've got to take a wicket or two.

Time to show that you're the best,
You've got to take a wicket or two.

When a side's batting well,
Time to act, give them hell.
Show them some pace, get in their face,
And go and take a wicket or two...
You've got to take a wicket or two, boys;
You've got to take a wicket or two.

Show them pace, get in their face,
Go and take a wicket or two.

When you hear teams that say
They will win, come what may.
Muster your guys and tell them straight,
You've got to take a wicket or two...
You've got to take a wicket or two, boys;
You've got to take a wicket or two.

Get your guys and tell them straight,
You've got to take a wicket or two!

# SEVENTIES
# SPECIALS

## AND ON MY OWN, SAD TO SAY

It was just some hours ago
That I saw a lovely girl I know.
I promised myself to be myself,
I wanted so much to show
I'm aiming for the top, with no way I would stop,
An ambitious man with a well-made plan
With a view to going places.
But even as we spoke I was broken
Into pieces, she upped and went,
My time was spent,
I found myself in limbo.
I might as well go home,
Since I am on my own,
And on my own, sad to say.

When I think that just last night
All the drink had made me tight,
But I had a dream, well, more a scheme
To see my girl and put things right.
But with morning came the rain,
And I was in lots of pain,
Though I felt quite ill I just took a pill
And I then felt so much better.
Giving me some hope
That this dope could do some healing,
But when we met I cocked it up,
She said I had no feeling. So leaving with a sigh,
She left me high and dry,
And on my own, sad to say.

It seems that I'm not wanted any more,
And if I go and keep on trying
I'll end up crying.
What should I do? What should I do?

Reflecting on the past few days,
I've tried to think of many ways
To do all that I could and possibly should
To find a way through the maze.
But at thirty-five years old,
With a cough and stinking cold,
Never had a hope as I couldn't cope
With the things she was demanding.
Leaving me no choice as I voiced my own ambition,
And though I tried so very hard
We both knew our position.
She went off in the night,
Now I'm a sorry sight,
And on my own, sad to say.
And on my own, sad to say.

## ANOTHER KICK IN THE TEETH

We can't find no inspiration,
We can't find no ball control.
It seems we're doomed to relegation.
Fans please leave our lads alone,
Oi! Fans please! Leave our lads alone.
All in all it's just another kick in the teeth.
All in all it's just another kick in the teeth.

We just need some inspiration,
We just need some ball control.
We may be doomed to relegation.
But please leave our lads alone.
Oi! Fans please! Leave our lads alone.
All in all it's just another kick in the teeth.
All in all it's just another kick in the teeth.

## BRING ON THE CLOUDS

Isn't it poor?
Where is the rain?
There's not a drop in the ground,
Drought time again.
Where are the clouds?

Isn't this sad?
Farmers despair.
Desperately praying for rain,
None in the air…
Where are the clouds?
Bring on the clouds.

Just when we thought wet days were due,
Hoping that one day we'd see that the sky
wasn't blue.
Having to soak up the sunshine again and
again
Nice as it is…
We need the rain.

What a big farce!
Who is to blame?
I think the forecasters don't care…
They're all the same!
And where are the clouds?
Bring on the clouds.
Well, they never came.

Isn't it poor?
Should shed a tear.
Having no rain, it's the same thing every
year.
And where are the clouds?
Please bring on the clouds…
At least come next year!

# BERNIE (THE BIGGEST DUSTMAN IN THE WEST)

You remember poor ol' Ernie, how he met his Waterloo,
And how two-ton Ted from Teddington went off and married Sue?
Well, unbeknown to all of us, a few years earlier on,
A little lass from Leckhampton gave birth to Ernie's son.

She'd heard about poor Ernie and the way in which he died;
"I swear I'll get my vengeance on that baker's man," she cried.
For twenty years she held back tears and taught her son to be
The best refuse collector in the local UDC...

They called him Bernie... (Bernie)...
And he drove the biggest dust cart in the west.

Now Bernie and his mother thought the time had come at last
To go and find that baker and confront him with the past.
They searched the village where he lived and knocked from door to door,
And found he'd moved from twenty-two to number forty-four.

Then Bernie's mum said, "Hold it son, while we devise a plan.
The first thing we must go and do is pinch his baker's van."
So Bernie towed it down the road and pushed it in the river,
Then smiled and thought, "That's one round there that baker won't
deliver!"

That was Bernie... (Bernie)...
And he drove the biggest dustcart in the west.

Bern raced back to his mother who was standing by Ted's gate,
They started shouting foul abuse, and didn't have long to wait.
The front door slowly opened and old Ted came into view,
He looked them up and down and said, "Now who the hell are you?"

"You may well ask," said Bernie, "And now you're going to know
That I'm the son of Ernie!" Ted staggered back, "Oh no!
I simply can't believe it's true. That's rubbish!" he then said.
"No, this is!" Bern cried, tipping his load on Ted's new flower bed.

They called him Bernie... (Bernie)...
And he drove the biggest dust cart in the west.

Ted said, "Well, I'm a widower now, with nothing to my name,
Except my lovely daughter Lil," and from the house she came.
Her hair was long, her eyes were blue, her smile was beaming bright,
And for Bern up on his dustcart he just knew 'twas love on sight.

Their eyes were fixed together as she cried, "Please have a heart."
Then Bernie said, "Of course I will, just jump up on the cart."
And as they drove off hand in hand, Bern's mum went up to Ted,
"Forget the past, let's join them!" So the four of them were wed.

All thanks to Bernie... (Bernie)...
And he drove the biggest dust cart in the west!

## DON'T LET MY SON BE MAD WITH ME

I can't fight no more of your battles,
All your problems seem to change from day to day.
I'm getting old and getting ever weaker,
Sitting here and I wonder what to say.

You're too late to stop yourself from failing,
You took a chance but didn't get it right.
Then you mistook my efforts trying to help you,
Slammed the door and went off crying in the night.

Don't let my son be mad with me,
Although he tried so hard it's just a shame he couldn't see.
I tried so hard to help him with his life and set him free,
But losing everything then had my son being mad with me.

He can't find, no, the right and proper line,
But I'm still here, he knows the way I feel.
He'll ignore me just because he thinks that he knows best,
Though he has his faults, I'm hoping soon that he'll get real.

Don't let my son be mad with me,
Although he tried so hard it's just a shame he couldn't see.
I tried so hard to help him with his life and set him free,
But losing everything then had my son being mad with me.

## MY REPUTATION

People say that I'm a c-clown (Talkin' about my reputation)
Hoping that I'd get out of town (Talkin' about my reputation)
They stick their noses in the a-air (Talkin' about my reputation)
I don't give a damn, I just don't care (Talking about my reputation)
This is my reputation, this is my reputation baby!

Why don't you all g-g-go to hell! (Talkin' about my reputation)
And take your snotty airs as well (Talkin' about my reputation)
You all lead me a merry d-d-dance (Talkin' about my reputation)
Never give me a second chance (Talkin' about my reputation)
This is my reputation, this is my reputation baby!

Never did anything right I kn-know (Talkin' about my reputation)
Messing things up and much too slow (Talkin' about my reputation)
It all boils down to my f-frustration (Talkin' about my reputation)
Talkin' about my reputation! (Talkin' about my reputation)
This is my reputation, this is my reputation baby!

Why don't you all g-g-go to hell! (Talkin' about my reputation)
And take your snotty airs as well (Talkin' about my reputation)
You all lead me a merry d-d-dance (Talkin' about my reputation)
Never give me a second chance (Talkin' about my reputation)
This is my reputation, this is my reputation baby!

People say that I'm a c-clown (Talkin' about my reputation)
Hoping that I'd get out of town (Talkin' about my reputation)
They stick their noses in the a-air (Talkin' about my reputation
I don't give a damn, I just don't care (Talkin' about my reputation)
This is my reputation, this is my reputation baby!

## HANDLE ON THE TEAM

Goodbye David Moyes,
Though we never knew why you came.
You thought you had just what it takes
While others kept away.

They stayed out of the running
While Sir Alex opted for you.
He offered you a fortune
Just to see what you could do.

And it seems to all you never did
Get a handle on the team;
Never knowing who to play where,
You ran out of steam.

And we all thought you would have listened
But you would have your way.
Your time is up and you must go,
There's nothing else to say.

Management is tough,
You took it on but I'm afraid
The job was quite simply too big for you,
The sack is the price you paid.

Even when you won,
How the press still hounded you
And the papers always said
That your days in charge of the team were through.

And it seems to all you never did
Get a handle on the team;
Never knowing who to play where,
You ran out of steam.

And we all thought you would have listened
But you would have your way.
Your time is up and you must go,
There's nothing else to say.

Goodbye David Moyes,
Though we never knew why you came.
You thought you had just what it takes
While others kept away.

Goodbye David Moyes,
Did you think that you could succeed
With changing line-ups every game;
I think that's quite naïve.

And it seems to all you never did
Get a handle on the team;
Never knowing who to play where,
You ran out of steam.

And we all thought you would have listened
But you would have your way.
Your time is up and you must go,
There's nothing else to say.

Your time is up and you must go,
There's nothing else to say.

## I DON'T LIKE SUNDAYS

The thumping head that I get when I wake
Is my fault from the night before.
As I feel like death and my hands both shake,
I don't think I can take any more.
It's the same thing every weekend,
Why it happens I don't know.
And I see no reason
'Cause there is no reason
The reason is I'm feeling low...

Tell me why?
I don't like Sundays.
Tell me why?
I don't like Sundays.
Tell me why?
I don't like Sundays.
I want to shoo
Them out of town.

The morning starts with a trip to the loo
As I'm feeling quite unwell.
And I look for the pills, well wouldn't you?
Without them I'd be worse than hell.
But just when I'm feeling better,
There's nowhere I can go,
And I see no reason
'Cause there is no reason,
The reason is I'm feeling low...

Tell me why?
I don't like Sundays.
Tell me why?
I don't like Sundays.
Tell me why?
I don't like Sundays.
I want to shoo
Them out of town.

The days get worse when the kids play rough
And go breaking all their toys.
Then the wife goes mad, and if that's not enough,
The shouting starts; I can't stand the noise.
There's nothing to do but bear it,
Doesn't matter how I try,
And I see no reason
'Cause there is no reason,
What reason do you need to cry?

Tell me why?
I don't like Sundays.
Tell me why?
I don't like Sundays.
Tell me why?
I don't like Sundays.
I want to shoo
Them out of town.

# I'M GLAD IT ISN'T CHRISTMAS EVERY DAY

When the postman brings the mail
Through the wind and snow and hail,
And you find you end up throwing most away.
Some are cards from ones you know,
But the others they can go.
You should check your list
To see which ones you've missed have come your way.

Well I'm glad it isn't Christmas every day,
It's a lot of work no matter what you say.
Oh, I'm glad it isn't Christmas every day,
Thank the Lord today's not Christmas.

When we're drinking at a bar
And we haven't come too far,
Then the atmosphere is really great in every way.
There are times there's too much noise,
When the booze gets to the boys.
It's the time we leave
And glad it doesn't happen every day.

Well I'm glad it isn't Christmas every day,
It's a lot of work no matter what you say.
Oh, I'm glad it isn't Christmas every day,
Thank the Lord today's not Christmas.

When the postman brings the mail
Through the wind and snow and hail,
And you find you end up throwing most away.
When the parcels weigh a ton (parcels weigh a ton)
Is it really lots of fun? (really lots of fun)
And the in-laws call you on the phone
To say they're going to stay.

Well I'm glad it isn't Christmas every day,
It's a lot of work no matter what you say.
Oh, I'm glad it isn't Christmas every day,
Thank the Lord today's not Christmas.

Okay you lot – fake it!


Well, I'm glad it isn't Christmas every day (every day)
It's a lot of work no matter what you say (say)
Oh, I'm glad it isn't Christmas every day,
Thank the Lord today's not Christmas.

Are you not glad each day's not Christmas?

# SIXTY WAYS TO PEEVE YOUR MOTHER

The question is what you have to do to make things bad.
The answer is simple though you'll make someone quite mad.
And I can help you with ideas that I once had.
There must be sixty ways to peeve your mother.

She's gone and caused you heartache each and every day,
And so I trust that my advice will help in some small way.
It's obvious the time has come you think that she must pay.
There must be sixty ways to peeve your mother.
Sixty ways to peeve your mother.

You just stay out all night, Dwight,
Stay in your bed, Ted,
You keep taking the pill, Jill,
And make her real mad.
Make yourself sick, Mick,
And don't miss a trick, Rick,
Keep on being rude, Jude,
And make her real mad.

You say she goes and makes your life a living hell.
I know there's lots that I can do, I think you know as well.
I've counted up the ways as far as I can tell.
There must be sixty ways.

I said why don't you all just think of what to do,
And once you've made your mind up you have got to see it through.
Your mother, she won't like it, so I guess it's up to you.
There must be sixty ways to peeve your mother.
Sixty ways to peeve your mother.

You just stay out all night, Dwight,
Stay in your bed, Ted,
You keep taking the pill, Jill,
And make her real mad.
Make yourself sick, Mick,
And don't miss a trick, Rick,
Keep on being rude, Jude,
And make her real mad.

# PORTERLOO

Oh my, a porterloo is something we must get hold of.
Oh yes, without a loo the crowds who come would be in
some discomfort.
Experience says it's a must;
Something in which we can trust.

Porterloo, when people need it, it's always there.
Porterloo, something you need to have at every fair.
Porterloo, need it for the likes of me and you.
Porterloo, actually we would need quite a few.
Wo, wo, wo, wo,
Porterloo, everyone needs a good porterloo.

Sometimes, I try to hold it back but can't wait longer,
Oh yes, and then I hope to find my way and fight through
all the crowds
And pray that I get there in time.
Relieving myself is sublime!

Porterloo, when people need it, it's always there.
Porterloo, something you need to have at every fair.
Porterloo, need it for the likes of me and you.
Porterloo, actually we would need quite a few.
Wo, wo, wo, wo,
Porterloo, everyone needs a good porterloo.

So pray that you get there in time.
Relieving yourself is sublime!

Porterloo, can be relied on the whole day through.
Porterloo, whether you need a wee or a poo!
Porterloo, actually we would need quite a few.
Porterloo, need it for the likes of me and you.
Whoa, whoa, whoa, whoa,
Porterloo, everyone needs a good porterloo.

## YOUR FRIEND DAN

Your friend Dan is a dirty old man,
Oh yeah, oh yeah.
He likes to read soft porn when he gets up at dawn,
Oh yeah, ah ha.

But in his way he caught your eye,
You can ignore him if you try.
I know that you would never lie,
But he is getting to you,
Getting to you.

Your friend John is an absolute con,
Oh yeah, oh yeah.
He's a miserable cheat whom I don't want to meet,
Oh yeah, ah ha.

But in his way he caught your eye,
You can ignore him if you try.
I know that you would never lie,
But he is getting to you,
Yes getting to you.

Your friend Joe is a drunkard you know,
Oh yeah, oh yeah.
He likes to drink all night till he's totally tight,
Oh yeah, ah ha.

But in his way he caught your eye,
You can ignore him if you try.
I know that you would never lie,
But he is getting to you.
He is getting to you.
He is getting to you.
He is getting to you.
Oh yeah.

# SANDS OF BRIGHTON

Are you just an old man
Who likes a sunny seaside,
Paddling in the water or lying on the sand?
Doing nothing else but laze,
Soaking up the gamma rays,
Hoping you end up with body nice and tanned.

So why don't you tell me your story?
And say to me why you feel so fine.
Let me shake you by the hand
And join you on the sands of Brighton.
I'd best be leaving before I change my mind.

Are you with somebody
There on the sands of Brighton?
Or are you loving life there all on your own?
There's no need for much thinking,
Just have more time for drinking.
If I come and join you, you won't be alone.

So why don't you tell me your story?
And say to me why you feel so fine.
Let me shake you by the hand
And join you on the sands of Brighton.
I'd best be leaving before I change my mind.

Have you tried their chip shops,
By the dozen on the seafront?
Best with salt and vinegar, fish galore.
Washed down with a pint of beer
Or anything that brings you cheer.
If one's not enough you can always ask for more.

So why don't you tell me your story?
And say to me why you feel so fine.
Let me shake you by the hand
And join you on the sands of Brighton.
I'd best be leaving before I change my mind.

And have you seen the old pier
In all its former glory,
Stretched across the sand and out to the sea?
Music playing everywhere
And no-one with a worldly care.
You're really very lucky and I do wish it was me.

So why don't you tell me your story?
And say to me why you feel so fine.
Let me shake you by the hand
And join you on the sands of Brighton.
I'd best be leaving before I change my mind.

# T-E-R-E-N-C-E

Now I'm going to tell you a pitiful tale
Of a man who is here tonight.
It might appear crude and a little bit rude
But I guarantee the facts are right.
I'm not going to keep you all guessing too long
'Cause I know that you'd very soon see,
I'm talking about the fanciful
T-E-R-E-N-C-E.

Well T-E-R-E-N-C-E
Has a birthday coming his way.
This may sound queer but for many a year,
He's always seemed happy and gay.
To see his furry legs and the hair on his lip
I don't think that you'd ever guess,
He likes to dress in women's
C-L-O-T-H-E-S.

These C-L-O-T-H-E-S
Include wearing high-heeled shoes.
When he's dressed in drag he resembles a bag,
And you know he can't hold his booze.
You can't call him Q-U-I-E-T
And you'd never say he was shy.
If he had his way he would snoop all day
As he's N-O-S-E-Y.

The A-L-C-O-H-O-L
Plays a major part of each day.
When he's not on the booze, he puts up with brews
And a cup of T-E-A.
It's so nice to know he can take a good joke
As anyone here can see.
We wish you a Happy Birthday
T-E-R-E-N-C-E.

# A CHRISTMAS CRACKER

# THE DAY AFTER CHRISTMAS

'Twas the day after Christmas and all through my head
Was a pounding so great that I thought I was dead.
I wondered what hit me and started to think
That it might have been something to do with the drink.

The rest of the family was still fast asleep
When I fell out of bed and then started to creep
To the bathroom, but suddenly had to be quick,
As I only just made it before I was sick.

A wash of my face started making things clearer,
A dab with a towel, then I looked in the mirror.
What stared back at me was a terrible sight,
The result of what happened the previous night.

The day's celebrations had all gone so well,
My wife and the kids loved it all, I could tell.
The presents, the tree and the games that we played,
Not forgetting the lunch that my dear wife had made.

But then came the evening when neighbours dropped in,
With the whisky, the brandy, the beer and the gin.
How much I had drunk I don't know, but it's said,
That it took several people to put me to bed.

So Boxing Day morning arrived all too soon
And it must have been dark; I could still see the moon.
I needed hot coffee, so started to go
Down the stairs, but I tripped and I stubbed my big toe.

But once in the kitchen I started to settle
And very soon made it to fill up the kettle.
The coffee worked wonders, and to my delight
I soon started to feel much more cheerful and bright…

…That didn't last long, as I very soon found
All the bottles and glasses still lying around.
The lounge was a mess, not a thing had been cleared,
But then would you believe: a good fairy appeared!

I'm joking of course, it was really my missus,
Who came down the stairs and she showered me with kisses.
"I'm glad you've recovered," then went on to say,
"What we have to do now is to clear this away."

Within half an hour the task was complete,
So we sat down for breakfast and something to eat.
The kids stayed in bed, but that gave us a break
From the terrible din that they usually make.

The morning passed quickly, the kids made a show,
And just before lunchtime it started to snow.
The sky had turned dark, it was ever so murky,
But inside was bright as we ate our cold turkey.

The afternoon saw us at war, playing games
Where the winner takes all, and I mention no names
But the person who ended the day number one
Wasn't me, nor my wife, but my number one son!

The snow had soon settled, so just before tea,
It was out to the back for a snowballing spree.
We loved every minute, got soaked to the skin,
But then tired and exhausted we ventured back in.

The evening passed quietly, I'm happy to say,
As we watched some TV and then called it a day.
And when all's said and done, I can say without fear,
Merry Christmas to all and a Happy New Year!

# ECSTATIC
# EIGHTIES

## A WINTER SALE

The days are shorter now, winter nights are closing in.
The question now is what to wear in all this weather,
It seems that I can never win.
The heating burns all day, my water bottle's always near,
But we look forward to what happens at the same time every year.

There is always a winter sale, thankfully a winter sale,
When we're on the search for bargains, I'm always first in line.
And I'm certain that you'll agree that it means a lot to you and me,
As you cannot fail whenever there's a winter sale.

The crowds form outside just waiting for the start of play,
I wonder if they know, I wonder if they're hoping
To get what they want on the day.
With luck I'll get there first, and it might mean that I jump the queue,
And there are times I might get mixed up in a fight,
But then wouldn't you?

There is always a winter sale, thankfully a winter sale,
When we're on the search for bargains, I'm always first in line.
And I'm certain that you'll agree that it means a lot to you and me,
As you cannot fail whenever there's a winter sale.

# I GUESS THAT'S WHY THEY BRING US THE NEWS

You've seen it today,
No doubt it will be on forever.
And as you can see they will go on and say
That things will never get better.
If they had their way
There would be nothing to hide.
It's been going on ever since time began,
And something we feel deep inside.

And I guess that's why they bring us the news,
From round the world here to me and to you,
Telling us stories, showing us places,
Scenes of destruction, pitiful faces,
And I guess that's why they bring us the news.

You've seen it before,
And yet there's more of the same.
Men who are fighting while others are dying,
It all gets reported each day.
We're all to blame
Wondering just what's going on,
Living each moment, just as we have done,
Since time in memoriam.

And I guess that's why they bring us the news,
From round the world here to me and to you,
Telling us stories, showing us places,
Scenes of destruction, pitiful faces,
And I guess that's why they bring us the news.

# I WANT WORK

I want work, but it's impossible.
A man like me, so reprehensible.
A man like me is downright lazy;
Other men say I'm quite crazy.

I can't work, I'm thick as hell;
Can't do nothing, and tired as well.
Never learnt a thing at school;
People say that I'm a fool.

But I want work, just an easy kind.
I want work, that pays a ton,
Won't tire me out, but feel like fun.
I want to work, that isn't too hard,
That's the work I want, I want work.

I want work on my own terms,
Though there's nothing I've ever learned.
Me, I'm useless and I'm slow,
Make a mess wherever I go.

So bring it on, but make it quick,
Don't give me work that makes me sick.
I only want an easy time,
A two-day week, that suits me fine.

But I want work, just an easy kind.
I want work, that pays a ton,
Won't tire me out, but feel like fun.
I want to work, that isn't too hard,
That's the work I want, I want work.

## I HAVE A SCHEME

I have a scheme, a plan in mind,
And at the end I hope to find
What could be a fortune if I get the sale.
I can see the future, and I mustn't fail.
I trust in my instincts,
Something I've believed in all these years.
I trust in my instincts,
And I haven't had the time for tears.
I'll back my team – I have a scheme.

I have a scheme, I've thought it through,
Not done before, it's something new.
It's my destination, daring to be bold,
Glad it's now all over, something to behold.
I trust in my instincts,
Something I've believed in all these years.
I trust in my instincts,
And I haven't had the time for tears.
I'll back my team – I have a scheme.
I'll back my team – I have a scheme.

## I'VE JUST CALLED TO SAY I'VE LEFT YOU

No words can say what must be said,
The wheels of fate are turning round inside my head.
No time to stall,
We've seen it all,
But time for me to go where angels fear to tread.

No joy for me, no last reprieve;
I tried to stay but now I've found it's time to leave.
I'm sad you know, but I must go,
I did my best for you, I hope you will believe.

I've just called to say I've left you.
I've just called to say a last goodbye.
I've just called to say I've left you.
But you will never know how much you broke my heart.

We had good times, as well you know,
And so it makes it very hard for me to go.
But now I find our love was blind
And over time I saw that it was all a show.

No comfort here, no more to say,
There's nothing you can do to make me want to stay.
It's time to fly, no time to cry,
And by the time you hear this I'll be miles away.

I've just called to say I've left you.
I've just called to say a last goodbye.
I've just called to say I've left you.
But you will never know how much you broke my heart.

Broke my heart...broke my heart.

# LOGICAL

I'm doing everything that I know I should,
Not needing your persuasion.
The things I do I know are good,
You see what I mean.
I listened to the things that you had in mind,
They didn't make much sense to me.
There's nothing more to think about,
I'd rather just let things be.

Let's think logical, logical,
We need to think logical, let's start thinking logical,
Time to get your mind to work, mind to work.
Time to get your mind to work.
Let's think logical, logical,
We need to think logical, let's start thinking logical.
Time to get your mind to work, mind to work.
Time to get your mind to work.

You're impatient, don't think straight,
Going in with all guns blazing.
I'm trying hard to get things done;
You don't seem to care.
I'm sure you understand how mad I get,
You're getting to me mentally.
You've got to get yourself together now,
And listen to my plea...

Let's think logical, logical,
We need to think logical, let's start thinking logical.
Time to get your mind to work, mind to work.
Time to get your mind to work.

Let's think logical, logical,
We need to think logical, let's start thinking logical.
Time to get your mind to work, mind to work.
Time to get your mind to work.

Or I'll get physical, physical,
I'm going to get physical, really mad and physical.
Time to get your mind to work, mind to work.
Time to get your mind to work.
Time to get your mind to work.

# RUNNING UP MY BILL

It really hurts me,
I suppose you know what it's like.
I suppose you feel the way I do about it,
I suppose you hate the thought of all you are spending.
Yes, both you and me.

And if they only would
Drop the price of their goods,
And we'd be better off with offers.
I'm running out of time,
I'm running up my bill,
I'm running out of money.
Hey, if only they would, oh...

They just try and fleece you
By keeping all their prices high,
Well aware they take you to the cleaners,
Ooh, they're as mean as anyone.

Do they really think of the heartache caused?
To them we don't matter do we?

Hey,
Both you and me,
Both you and me agree we're not happy.

And if they only would
Drop the price of their goods,
And we'd be better off with offers.
I'm running out of time,
I'm running up my bill,
I'm running out of money.
Hey, if only they would, oh...

Hey,
Both you and me,
Both you and me agree we're not happy.

Come now mister, come now mister,
Let us come to some arrangement now.
Oh please now mister, please now please now help me,
Let's arrange for a discount somehow.

And if they only would
Drop the price of their goods,
And we'd be better off with offers.
I'm running out of time,
I'm running up my bill,
I've got problems...

## YOU FLUFF IT

Every time I see you I'm a worried man.
Really wishing to avoid you if I can.
One look at you will spoil my day,
I pray that you will stay away.

Anything you do you fluff it,
Anything you try you fluff it,
Anything at all you fluff it,
Go away.

Every time you try your hand at something new,
Nothing ever works as you don't have a clue.
You live your life without a care,
Nobody needs you anywhere.

Anything you do you fluff it,
Anything you try you fluff it,
Anything at all you fluff it,
Go away.

I'm sad that you don't even try,
It seems that life will pass you by.
Anything you do you fluff it,
Anything you try you fluff it,
Anything at all you fluff it,
Go away.
Anything you do you fluff it,
Anything you try you fluff it,
Anything at all you fluff it,
Go away. Anything at all
Go away,
You fluff it!

## THE GREAT DEFENDER

Oh yes, I'm the great defender,
Defending with so much pride.
My game is such I defend so much;
I'm awesome, the best in my side.

Oh yes, I'm the great defender,
Just playing each match as it comes.
My team you see all depend on me,
We treat opposition like bums.

To me it's a matter of life and
death,
To me I feel better when I've
nothing left.

Oh yes, I'm the great defender,
I treat every side all the same.
I'm well renowned for hacking men
down,
To me it's all part of the game.

To me it's a matter of life and
death.

Oh yes, I'm the great defender,
I treat every side all the same.
I'm well renowned for hacking men down,
To me it's all part of the game.
Defending's the name…
Defending's the name of the game.

# AND
# TO
# FINISH

## FRY ME SOME LIVER

I must say I'm starving,
You say you're hungry too.
Well, you can fry me some liver,
Fry me some liver,
I fried some liver just for you.

Yesterday was curry,
Very hot vindaloo.
So you can fry me some liver,
Fry me some liver,
I fried some liver just for you.

We argued, yes we argued the other day,
Over what, I can't recall.
Forget it, just forget it, and let me say,
The meal we had was not too sumptuous,
Still no cause to call me bumptious.

And now you say you're sorry,
So prove to me that you do.
Just try to fry me some liver,
I fried some liver just for you, just for you.

Now you say you're sorry,
So prove to me that you do.
Just try to fry me some liver,
I fried some liver just for you,
I fried some liver just for you.

# RAIN IS ALL AROUND

I see it in the fields, I see it on the roads.
Rain is all around us, and with nowhere to go.
It comes in with the wind, sometimes it comes as snow.
If anyone can hear me, we'd like it all to go.

The roads are flooded, rivers so wide;
Try to keep dry but there's nowhere to hide.
The rain keeps falling;
There seems no end.
With climate change, it's now the trend.

The rain first soaked my garden,
And now it's in my home.
It's ruined all the carpets,
And I feel so alone, oh yes I am.
I blocked the door with sandbags,
It then came through the floor.
I'm stuck here in my bedroom,
I can't take any more.

The roads are flooded, rivers so wide;
Try to keep dry but there's nowhere to hide.
The rain keeps falling;
There seems no end.
With climate change, it's now the trend.

When will it stop raining?

Oh it comes in with the wind,
Sometimes it comes as snow.
If anyone can hear me,
We'd like it all to go.

# I DID IT FOR ME

Listen up you guys, gather near,
I want you to hear.
Clear your heads, clear your minds
And when you're ready then I will proceed.

I tell you it's all worth sweating for,
I can tell you that I'm now getting more.
I trust you'll see
What will be will be, I did it for me.

Working for myself I soon found
My life had turned around.
Being on my own, I can sing,
Couldn't give a damn, wouldn't change a thing.

I tell you it's all worth sweating for,
I'm so happy now I'm getting more.
I trust you'll see
What will be will be, I did it for me. Oh yes!

There's no time like free time.
What I do now, it gives me time
To work hard and to play hard,
I'll always play the right card.

Why not try the same, you guys.

Oh, I can tell you it's all worth sweating for,
I'm so happy now I'm getting more.
Yes, I won't lie to you, won't cry for you,
Not inspired by you, I won't fly to you,

I trust you'll see
What will be will be, I did it for me.

# IT'S A TERRIBLE DAY

I can see why
You can't seem to control me
When I can't seem to handle myself.
And I can just see
That no-one wants to know me when I'm in this mood.
People beware; I've said before that there are times
When I get out of the wrong side of bed,
I'm not at my best,
And I often lose my mind, and lose my way.
You cannot really know
How I do suffer so
When I feel like this, I feel so sad.

Oh oh oh
It's a terrible day and I can't help myself from crying,
And I'm thinking that I'm dying,
And you may think that I'm lying.
It's a terrible day, the wind is up, and it's still raining,
And though I've had to miss my training,
Everything I do is draining,
And I'm sad that you have left and gone away,
It's a terrible day.

I want you to know that I love you so
But I'm weary, and knowing that I've been a fool
I'm not OK;
Done some stupid things before, even today.
You cannot really know
How I do suffer so.
I want you back where you belong.
I need you to come back soon, I know now that I've done wrong.

It's a terrible day and I can't help myself from crying,
And I'm thinking that I'm dying,
And you may think that I'm lying.
It's a terrible day, the wind is up, and it's still raining

And though I've had to miss my training,
Everything I do is draining,
And I'm sad that you have left and gone away.


For one day soon I know I'll wake up,
And I'll regret our little break-up,
But until your back with me and here to stay,
Then it's a terrible day.
Terrible day,
Oh, darling, not until you're here back to stay,
It's a terrible day.

# YOU JUST HAVEN'T MET ME YET

You're so surprised, you can't make things last,
You go breaking hearts all of the time.
You couldn't keep track, talked yourself up
Then let yourself down, you get all depressed, and you haven't a clue.
You try so very hard but you lose it,
You really don't have any excuses.
You think, you think you'll never meet a man like me!
But I know one day that you will come around,
You'll find a man who'll try to help you work things out.
The new love of your life, all the rest of your men you'll forget.
You just haven't met me yet.

As time passes by, you have to be strong,
It may be bad timing, and admit when you're wrong.
Wherever you go, whatever you do,
You have to keep going and see it all through.
I confess that I am simply amazing,
There is nothing you can't like about me.
Then you'll think you'll never meet another like me.
But I know one day that you will come around,
You'll find a man who'll try to help you work things out.
The new love of your life, all the rest of your men you'll forget.
You just haven't met me yet.

You've had your share of love and war
But be warned not to fight it.
Don't get uptight and don't be short-sighted.
For in time you will find that I'm so amazing,
And once I'm in your life I'm going to change you.
Then you'll think you'll never meet another like me.
And at last you know it's all for the best,
And we'll try our very best.
Rest assured now you'll get more with me yet,
With me yet, with me yet, with me yet.

Oh, for sure it'll all work out,
And you'll find a man who'll try to help you work things out.
Rest assured you will get so much more, more with me yet.
Yeah, you just haven't met me yet,
You just haven't met me yet.

Rest assured you will get so much more, more with me yet,
You'll find love, love, love,
Love, love, love, love.
(You just haven't met me yet)
Love, love, love, love,
Love, you just haven't met me yet.

**PRINTED AND BOUND BY:**

Copytech (UK) Limited trading as Printondemand-worldwide,
9 Culley Court, Bakewell Road, Orton Southgate. Peterborough,
PE2 6XD, United Kingdom.